# SOCIAL EMOTIONAL LEADERSHIP

| DIMENSIONS | ATTRIBUTES | DEFINITIONS |
|---|---|---|
| **Leading Self** | **Self-Aware** | can describe what makes them who they are |
| | **Accountable** | takes responsibility for their actions |
| | **Resilient** | keeps trying if they fail at an important goal |
| | **Integrity** | stands up for what they believe in |
| **Leading with Others** | **Collaborative** | cooperates with others effectively |
| | **Communicative** | expresses ideas clearly and effectively |
| | **Active Listener** | listens carefully to what others have to say |
| | **Considerate** | thinks about how their actions make other people feel |
| | **Respectful** | treats other people the way they want to be treated |
| | **Accepting** | appreciates the views of others, even if they are different from their own |
| **Changing Your World** | **Visionary** | creates a compelling vision and inspires others to follow it |
| | **Motivating** | unites a group of people to work together toward a common goal |
| | **Encouraging** | encourages others to take on leadership roles |
| | **Confident** | steps up and takes charge when it is needed |

# LEADING SELF

Deep understanding of yourself and your own behavior

Self-aware — Accountable — Resilient — Integrity

*"Leading Self means that I am self-aware of what is happening and how I feel. It means that I am growth-minded and open to new Ideas. It means that I am motivated in what I do. It means that I am resilient. It means that I am accountable."*

— Middle School Student

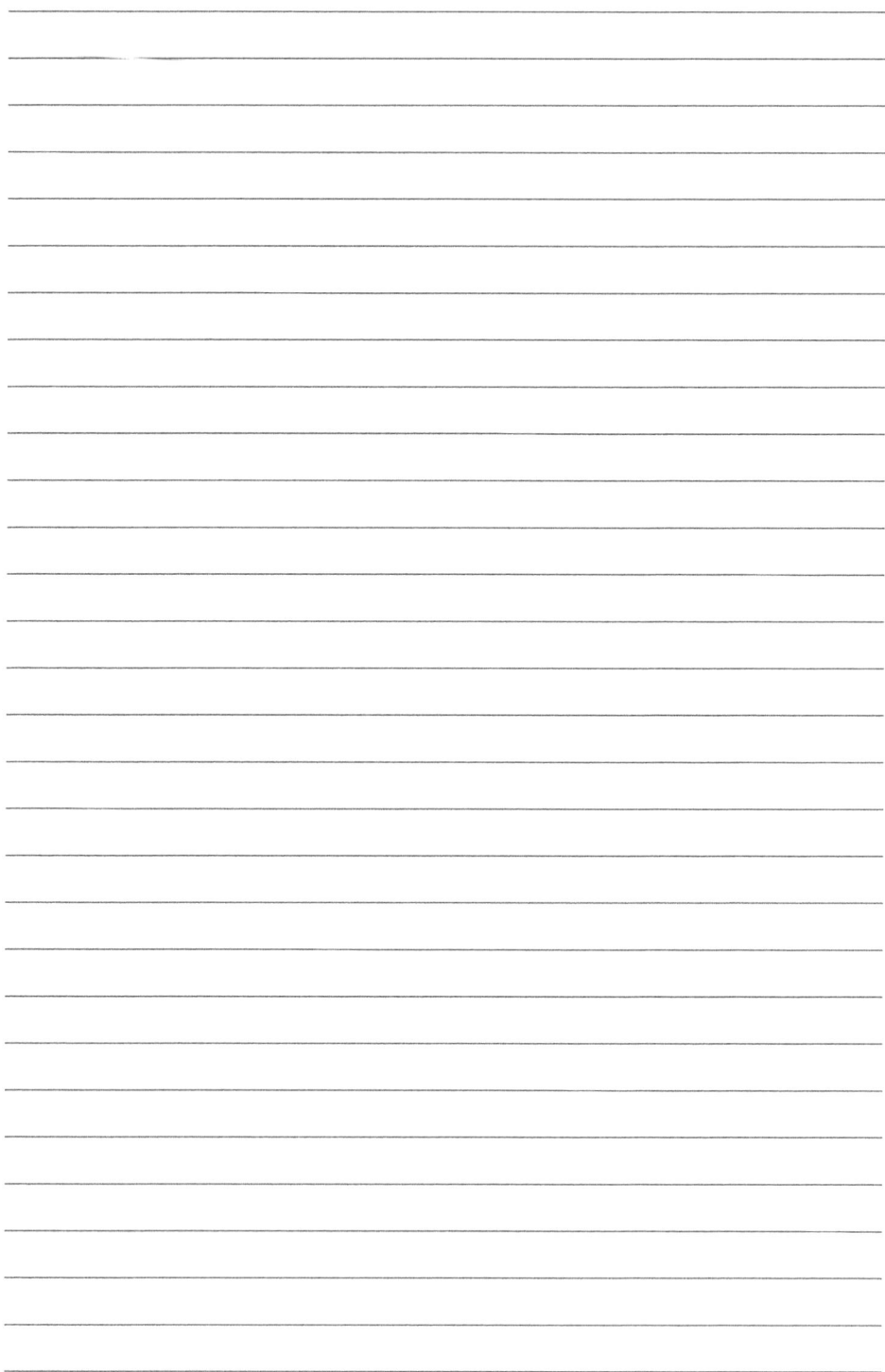

_____

_____

_____

_____

_____

_____

_____

_____

_____

_____

_____

_____

_____

_____

_____

_____

_____

_____

_____

_____

_____

_____

_____

_____

_____

_____

_____

_____

_____

*"Being self-aware is being able to control what you say and who you say it to."*

— Eighth Grade Student

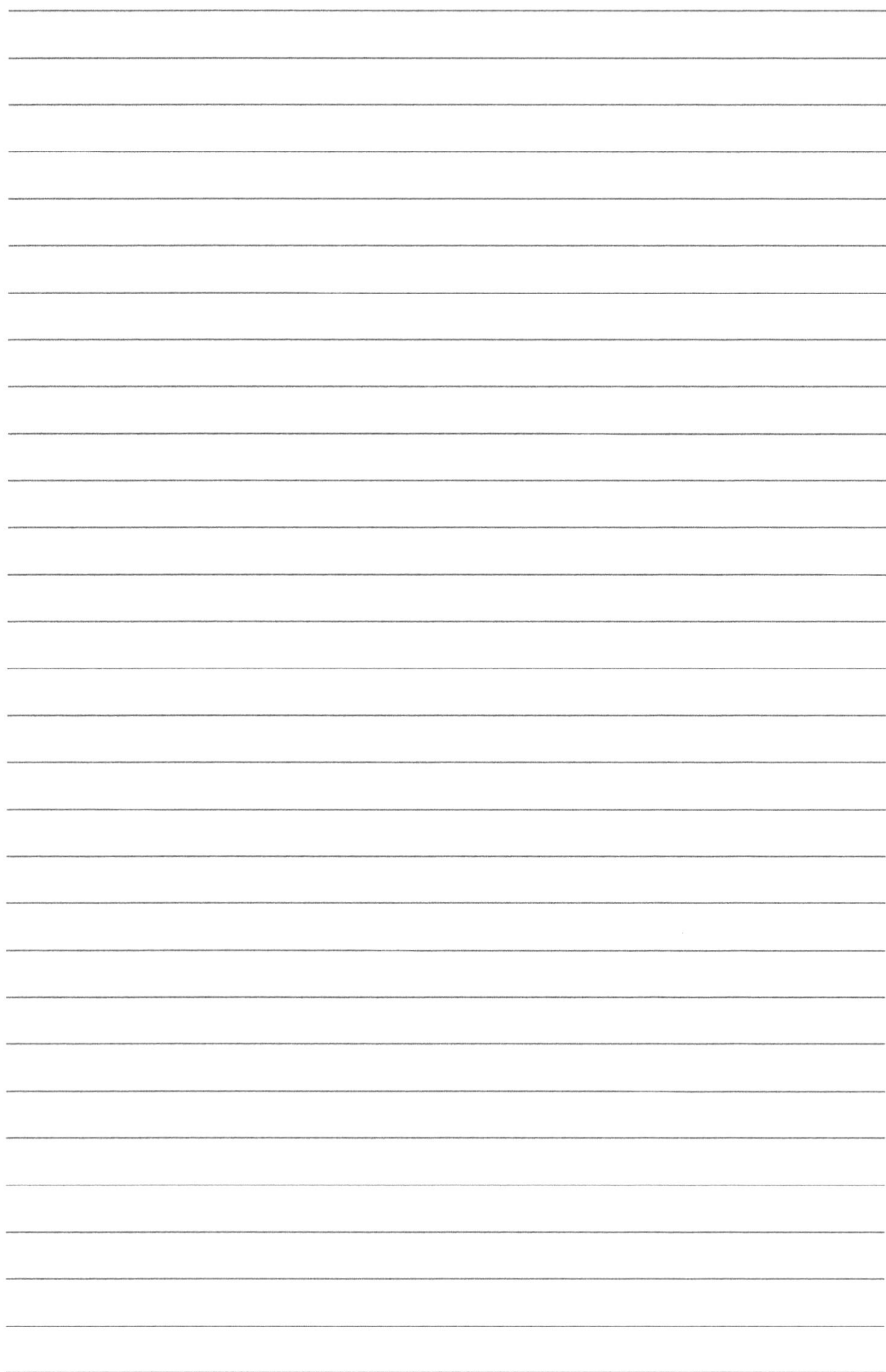

_"I am aware of both my negative and positive qualities and the areas where I am capable and the areas where I need help."_

— 12th Grade Student

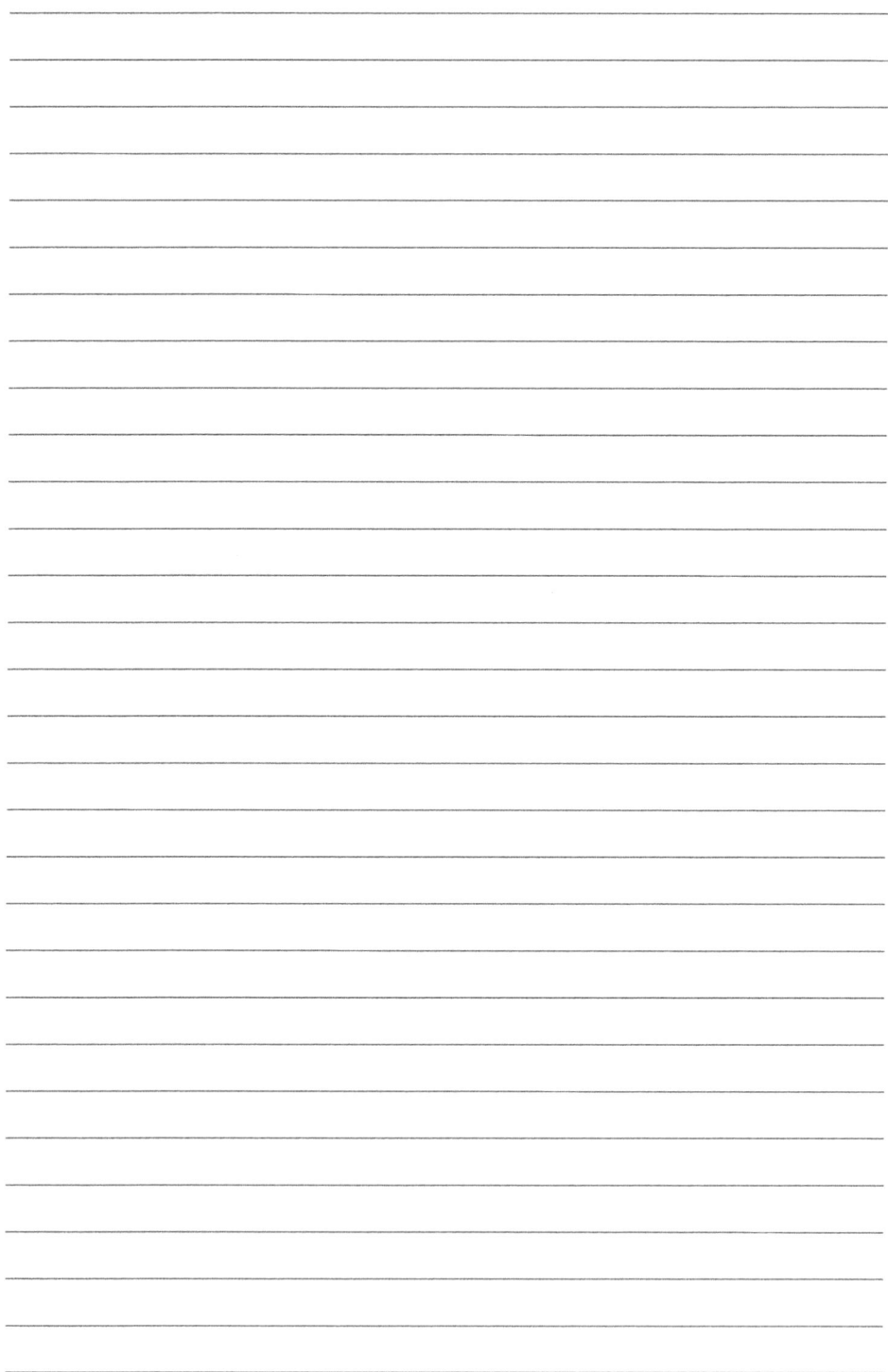

*"To me, accountable means that I have to be trustworthy and leading myself. Or, when you know that you did something wrong, you go and confess that you were the one because you know that was the right thing to do."*

— Fourth Grade Student

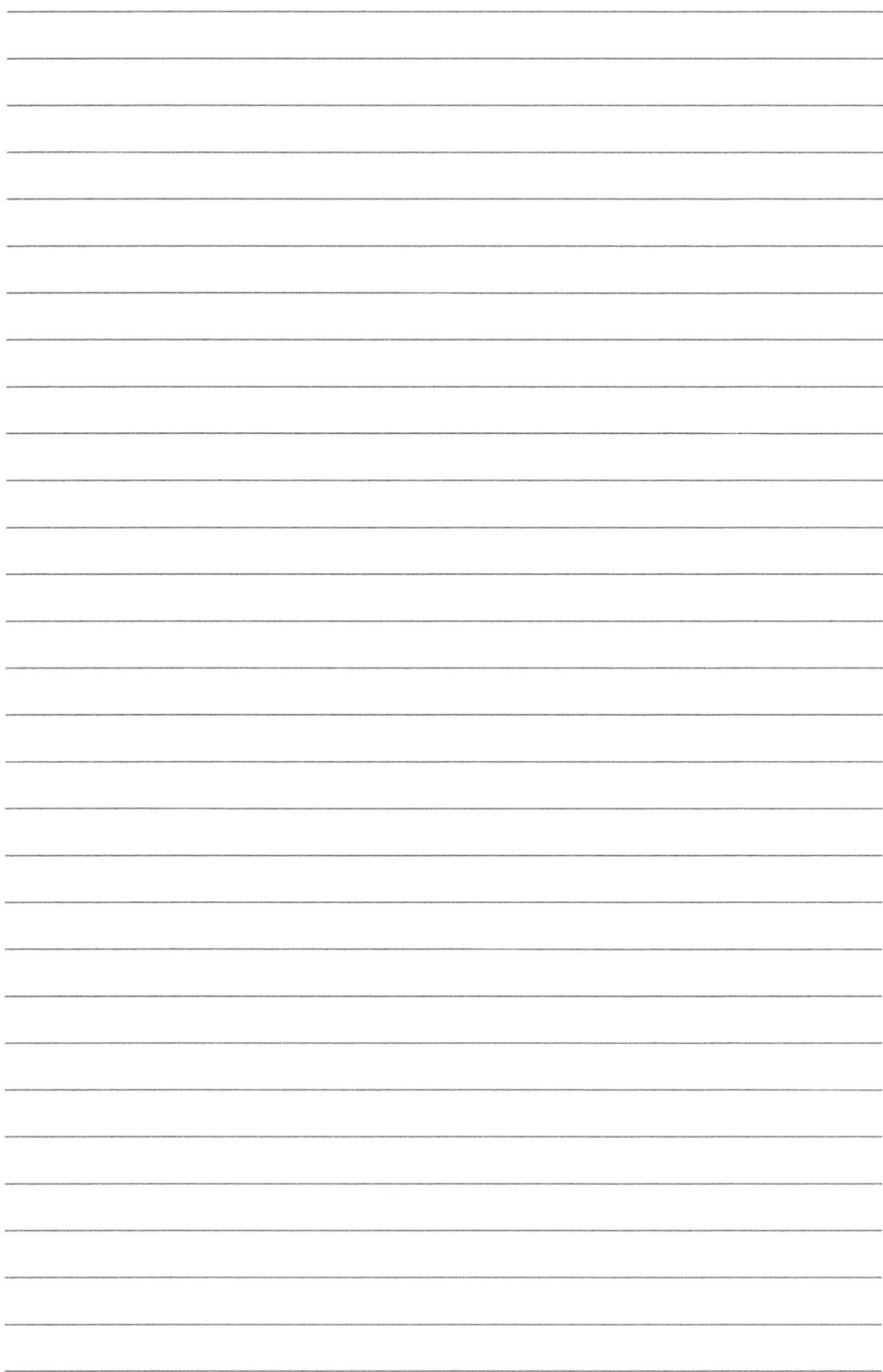

_"Being accountable to me means that you are responsible in remembering
things and that you are honest about things."_
— Seventh Grade Student

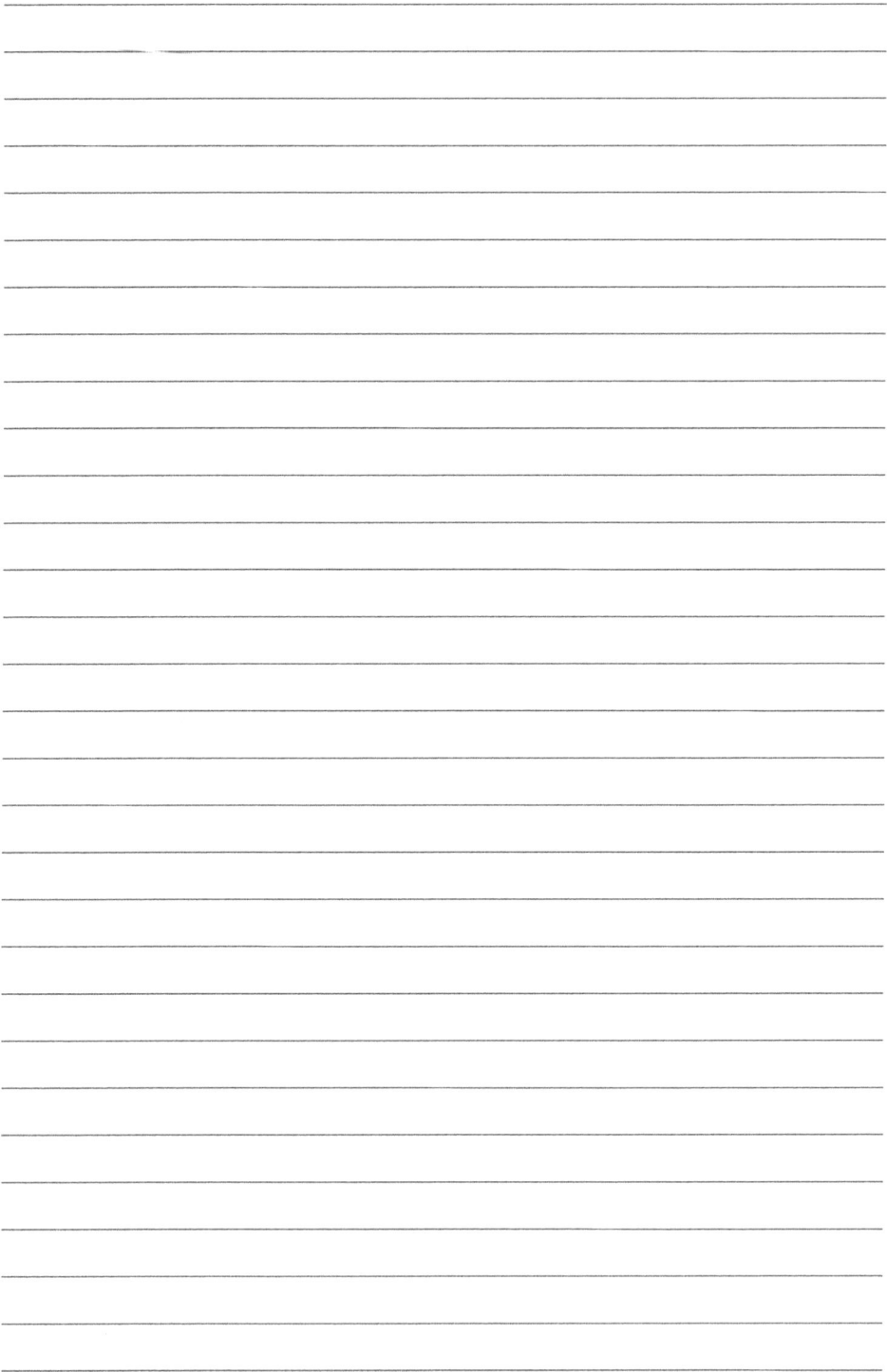

_"Being accountable means establishing a reputation of being good to rely on,
someone who does what they promise to do."_

— Ninth Grade Student

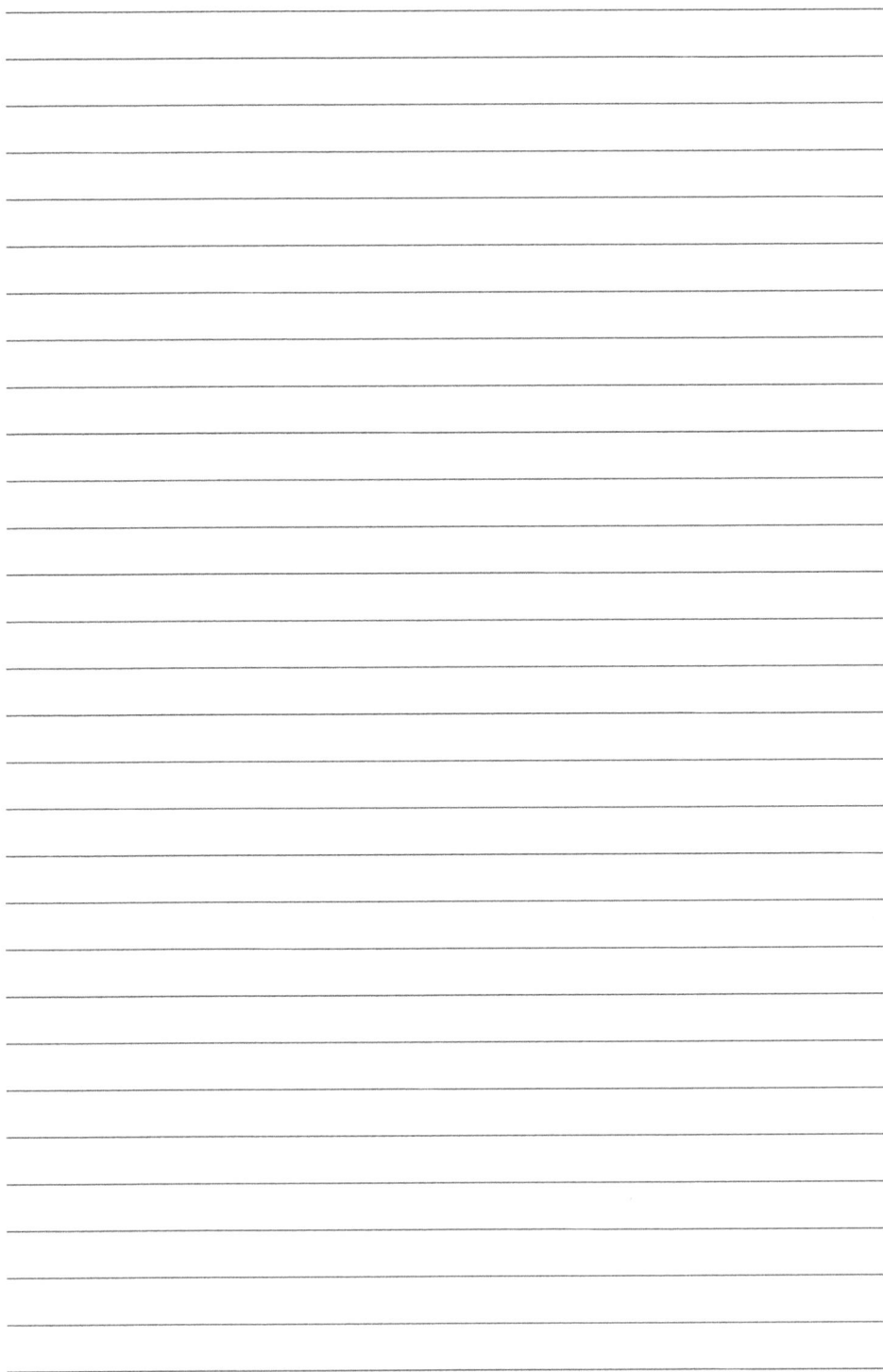

_"Resilient means to bounce back from a setback such as a bad grade on a test, or not winning a game."_

— Seventh Grade Student

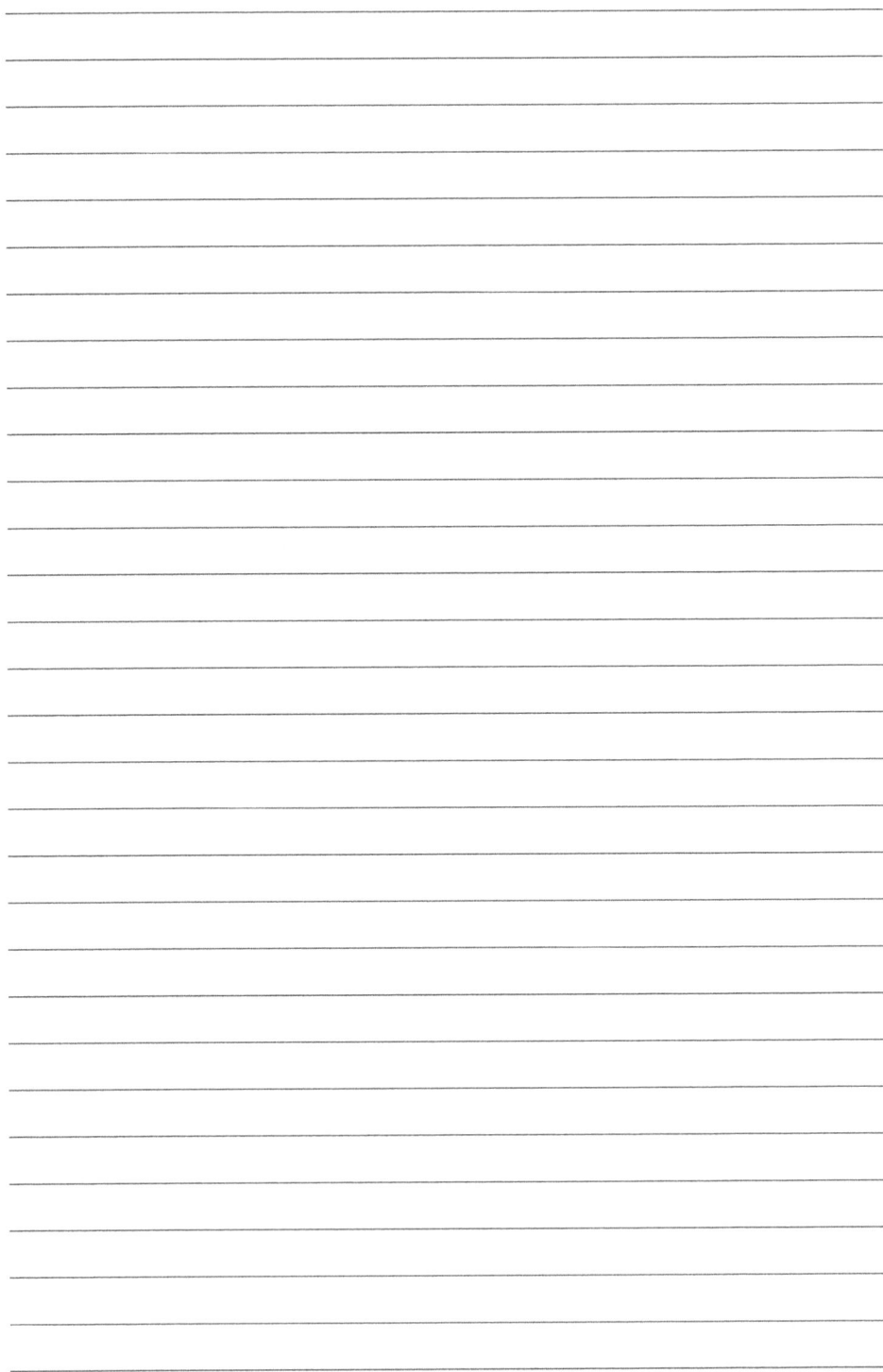

*"Being resilient means not letting life's obstacles and problems make you give up, but keep going even though it is hard."*

— 11th Grade Student

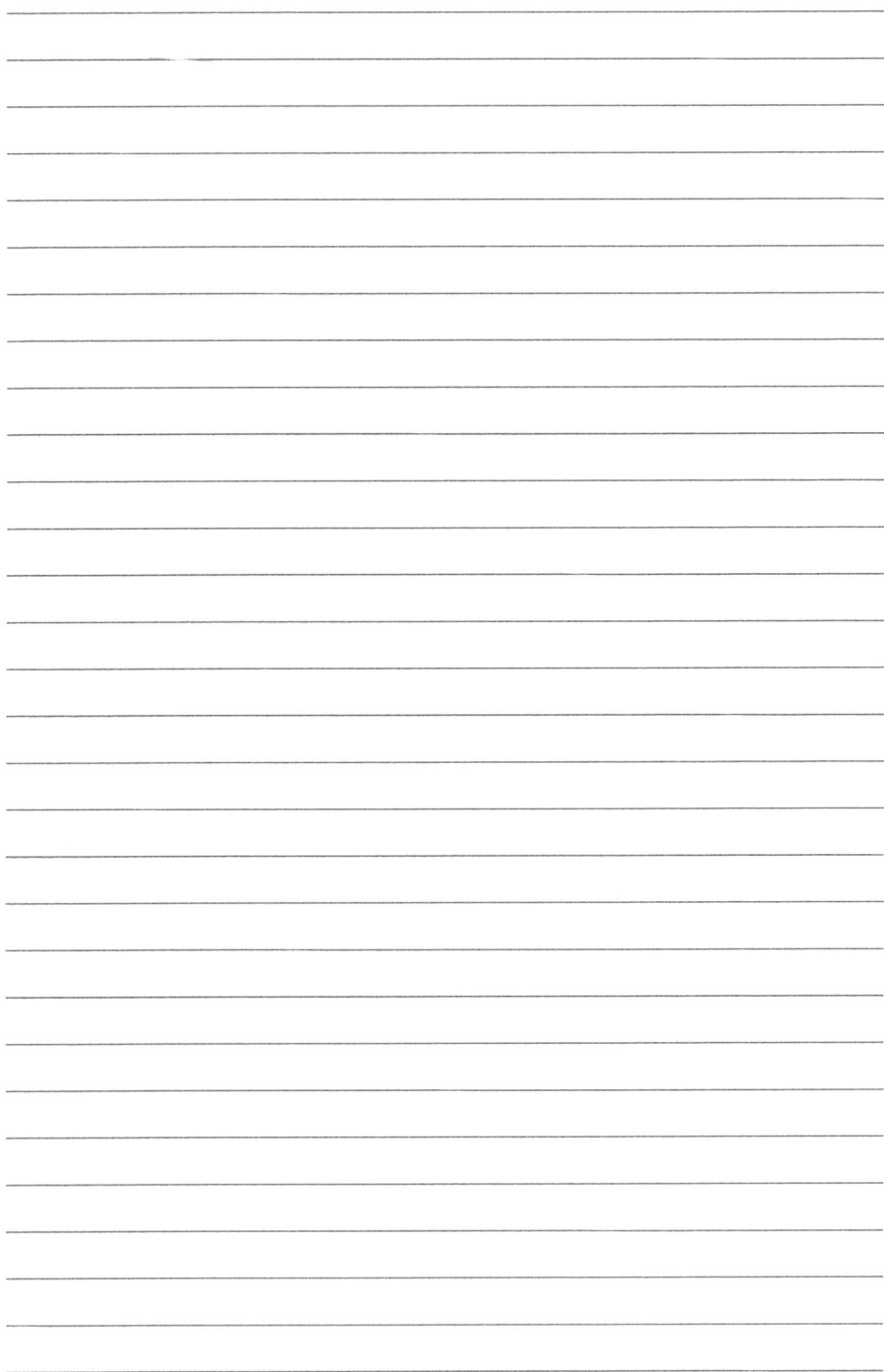

_____

_____

_____

_____

_____

_____

_____

_____

_____

_____

_____

_____

_____

_____

_____

_____

_____

_____

_____

_____

_____

_____

_____

_____

*"[Integrity] means that I am doing the right thing if someone is looking or not. I do what the person in charge says the first time, not the second time or more. It also means that I am listening and being aware of what the person is saying or doing. I do what the right thing is no matter if everybody else in the room is not doing the right thing. I make sure I take home the right supplies and turn work in on the correct due date."*

— Fifth Grade Student

# LEADING WITH OTHERS

Working effectively with others

Collaborative — Communicative — Active Listener
Considerate — Respectful — Accepting

*"Leading with others means always including and thinking about others never just yourself, everyone is important and you don't have to be the one in charge and shouldering everything, we can all work together."*

— High School Student

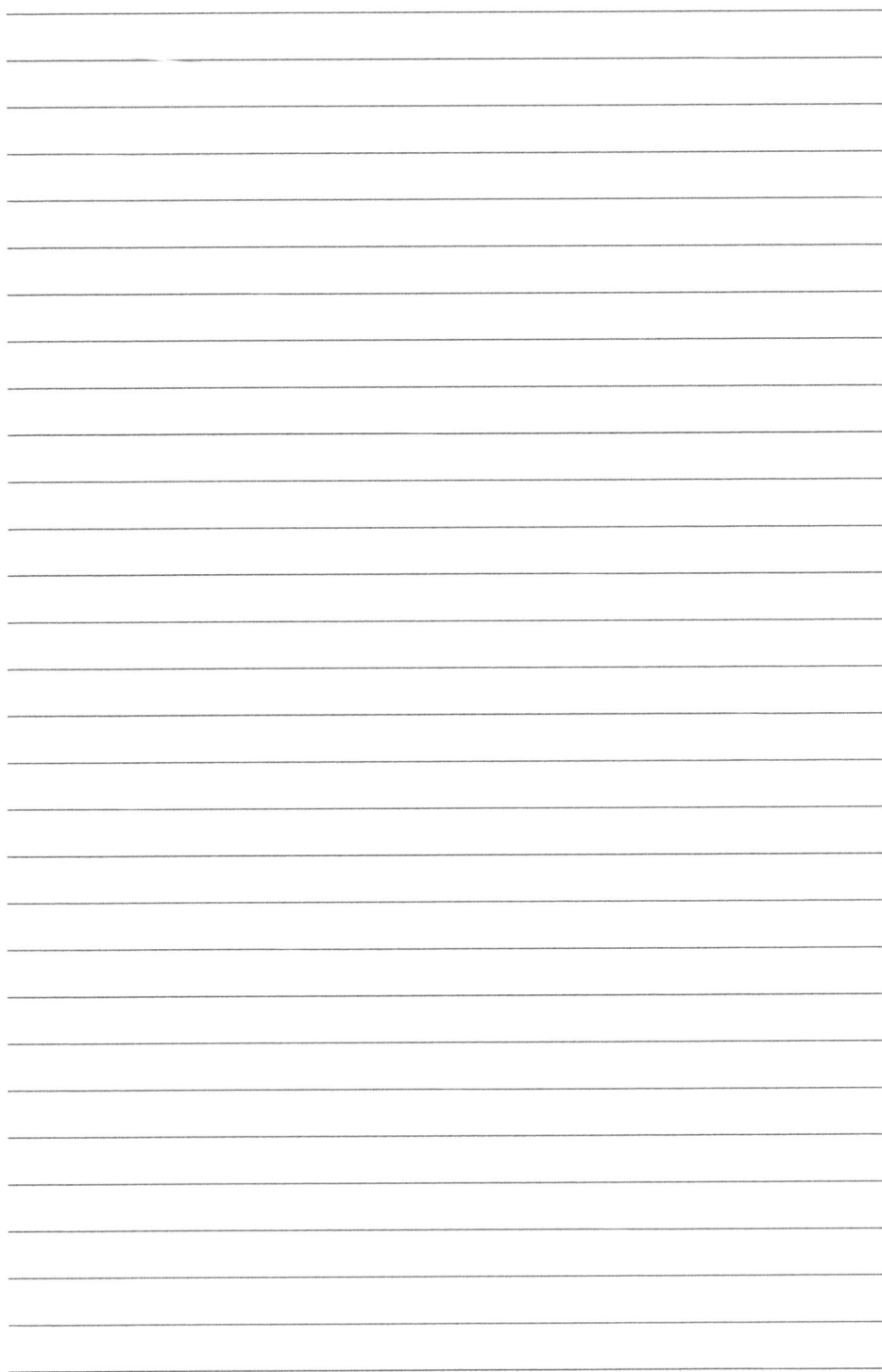

*"Collaborative means to me that you work with others to become a team.
I think that when you are collaborating that means to share ideas, use other
peers ideas and come up with one big idea to do together."*
— Fifth Grade Student

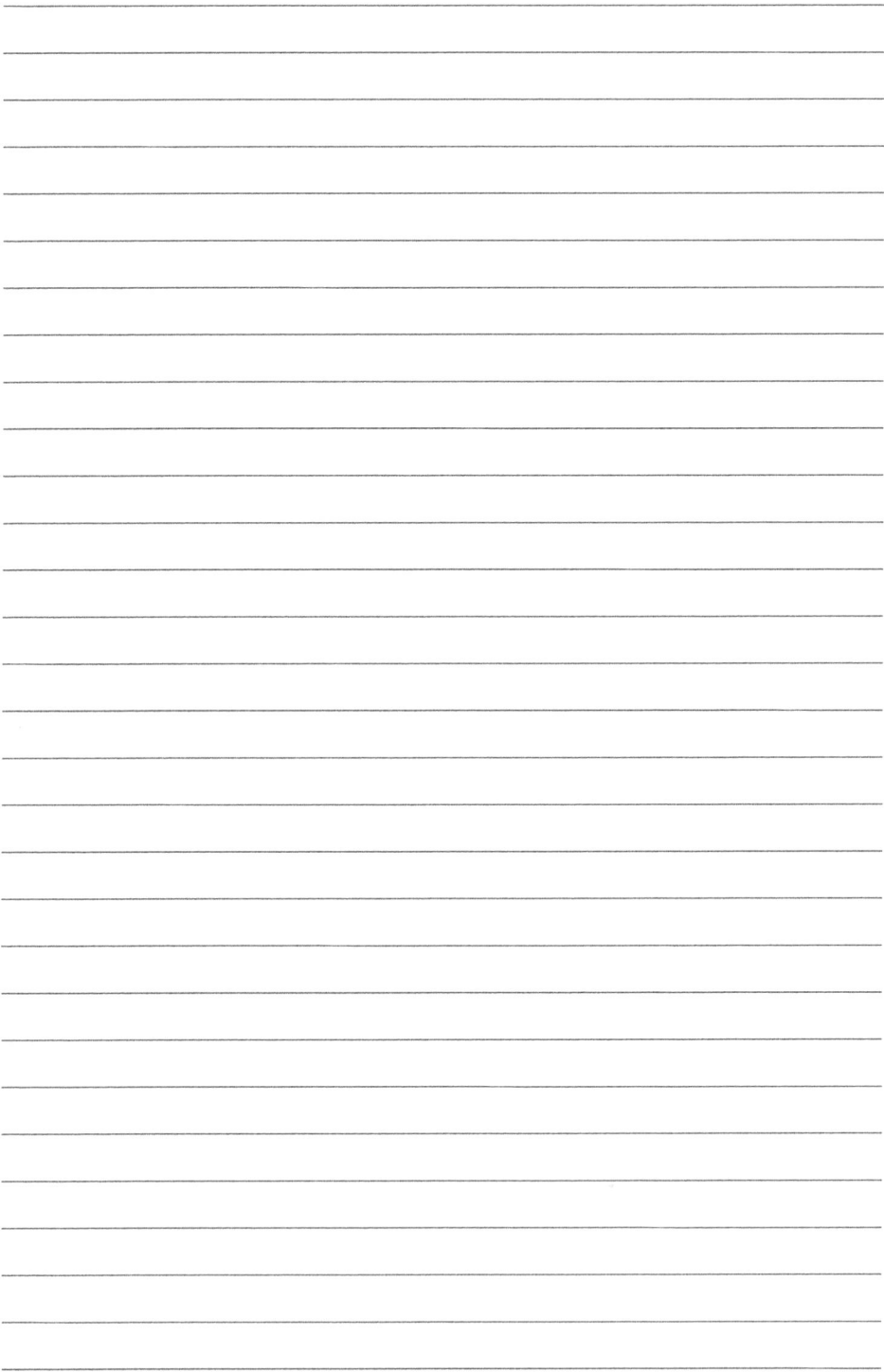

_____

_____

_____

_____

_____

_____

_____

_____

_____

_____

_____

_____

_____

_____

_____

_____

_____

_____

_____

_____

_____

_____

_____

_____

_____

_____

_____

_____

_____

_____

_____

_____

_____

_____

*"Being able to work well with others is very important. Listening to their ideas and finding what works best for a situation will make it have the best possible outcome."*

— Eighth Grade Student

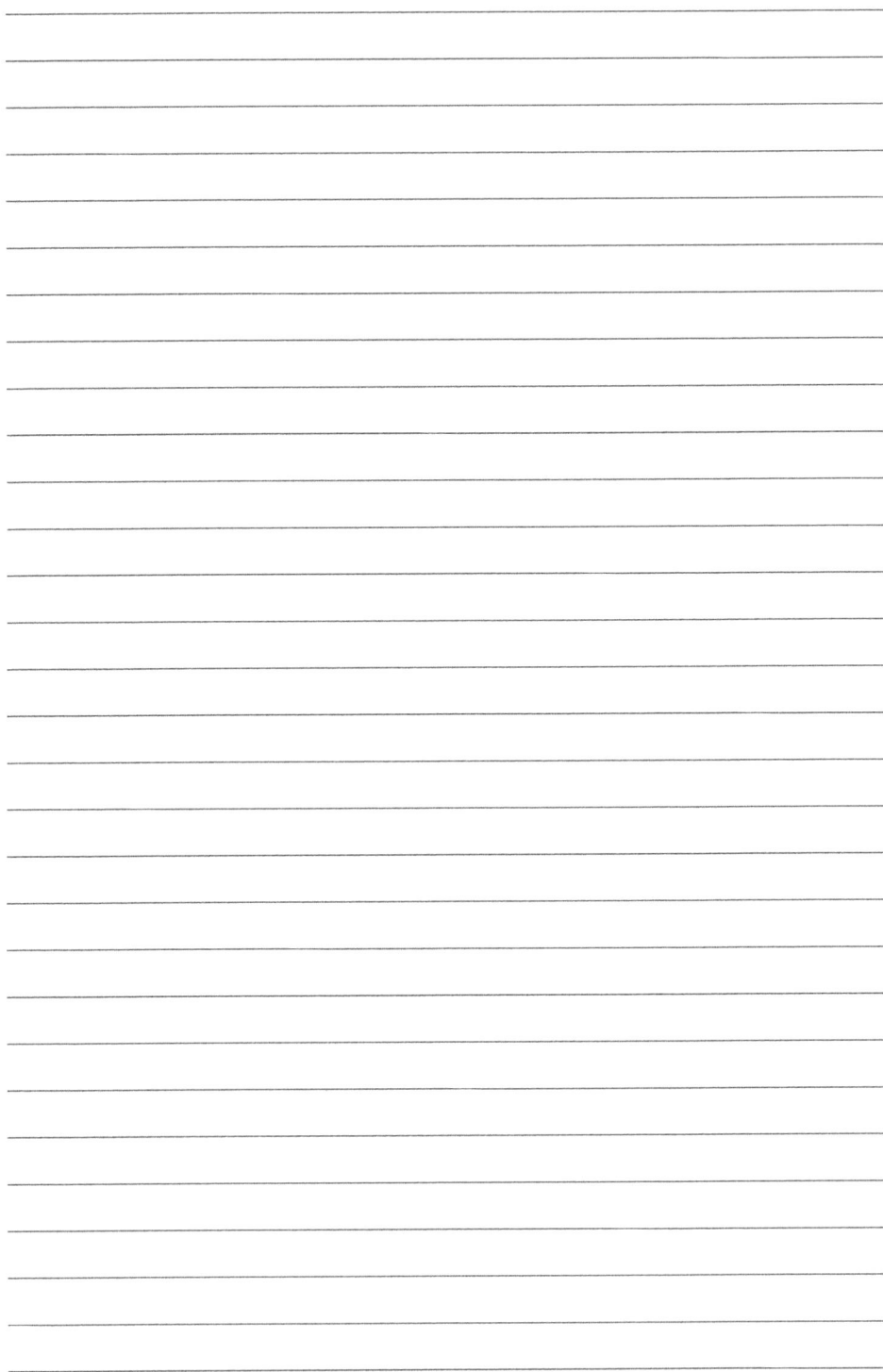

_"Collaborating means communicating with my peers to create and share ideas."_
— 10th Grade Student

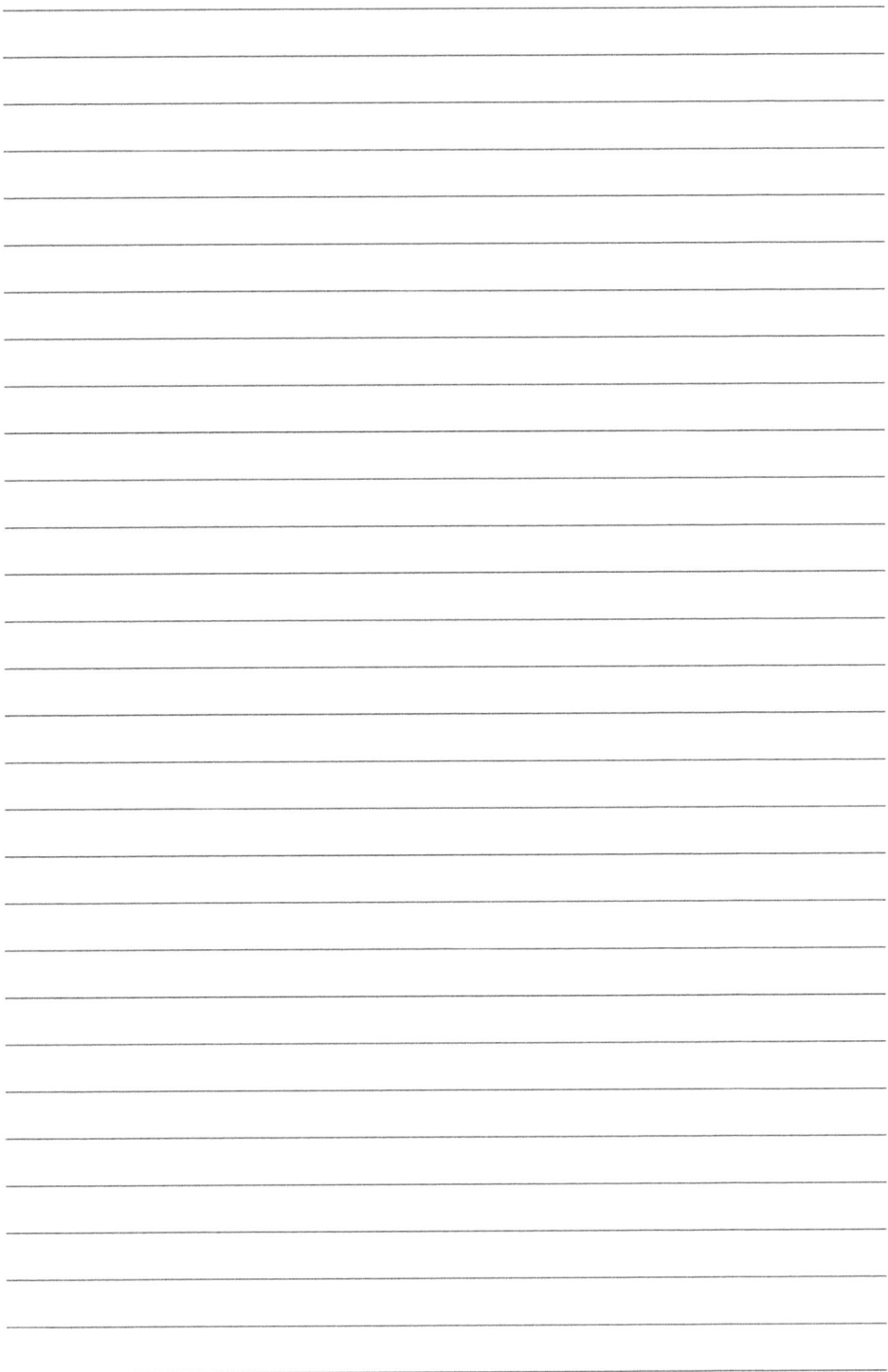

*"Being collaborative means being able to express feelings and opinions with others in order to move forward and improve."*

— 12th Grade Student

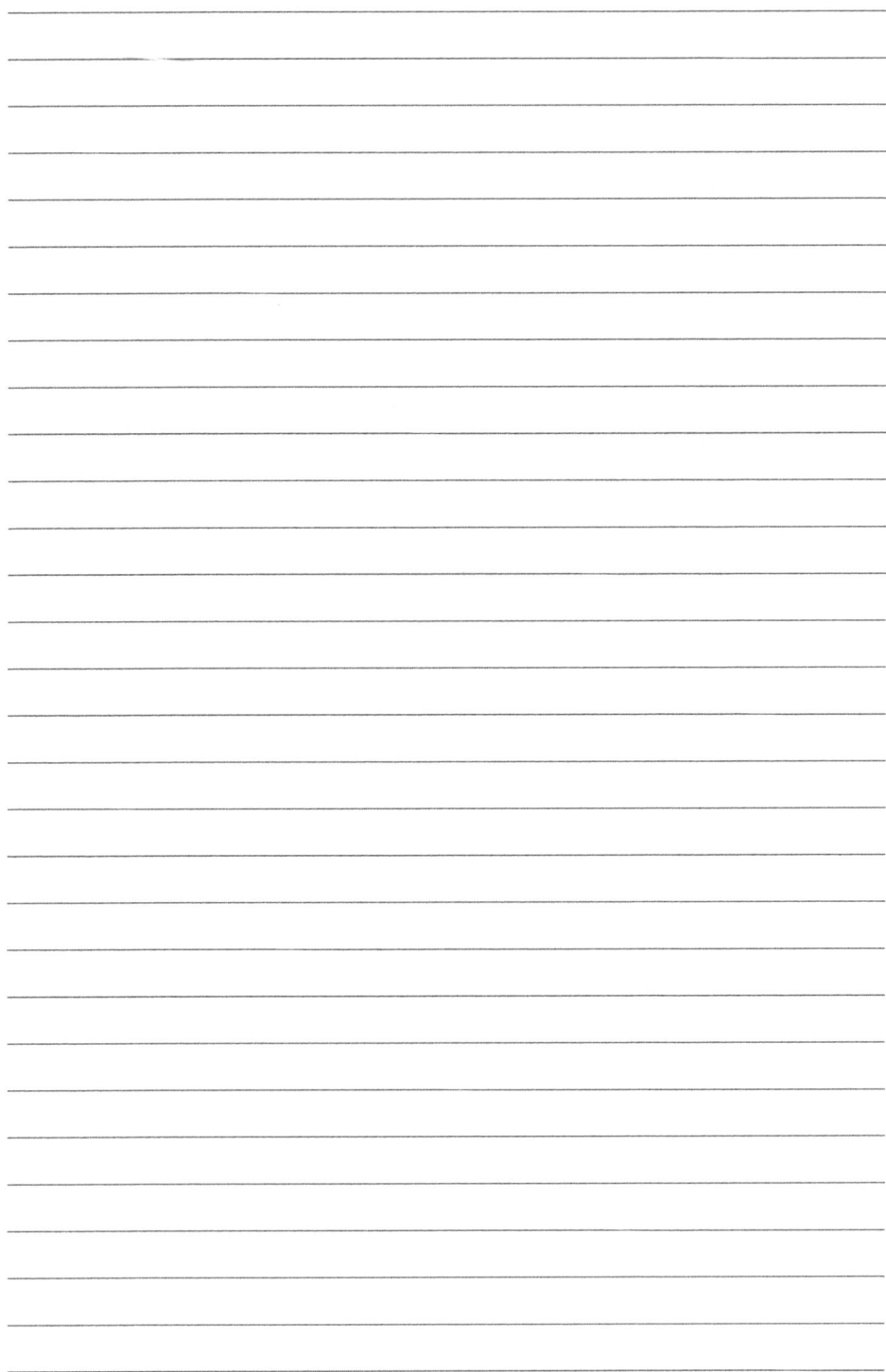

_____
_____
_____
_____
_____
_____
_____
_____
_____
_____
_____
_____
_____
_____
_____
_____
_____
_____
_____
_____
_____
_____
_____
_____
_____
_____
_____
_____
_____

*"Communicative means listen to each other and know what they mean
and what they are saying. And help explain what they're saying"*
— Third Grade Student

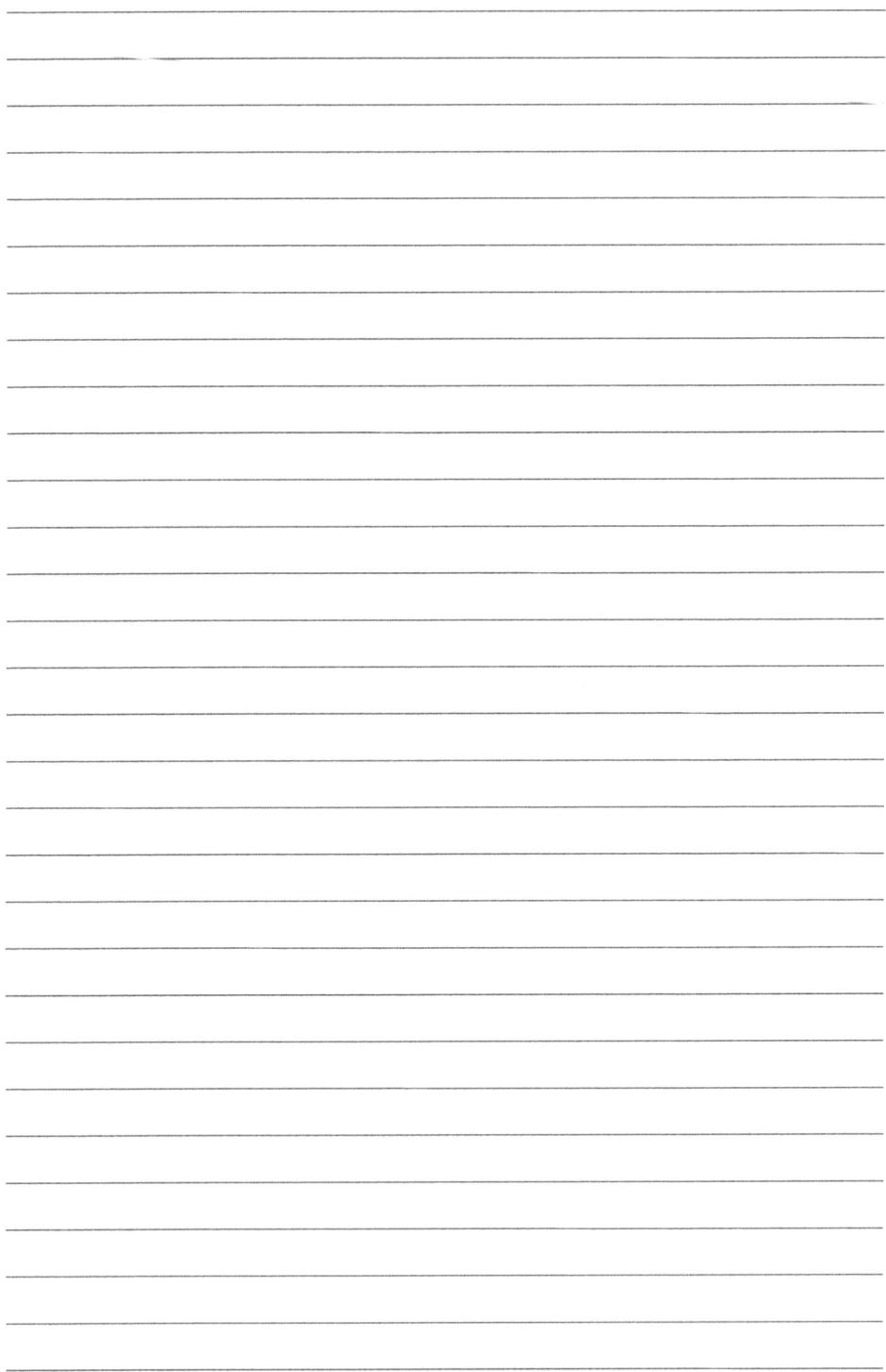

_"[Being communicative means] to tell people what you are thinking_
_and how we can do better as a unit to accomplish a similar goal."_
— Seventh Grade Student

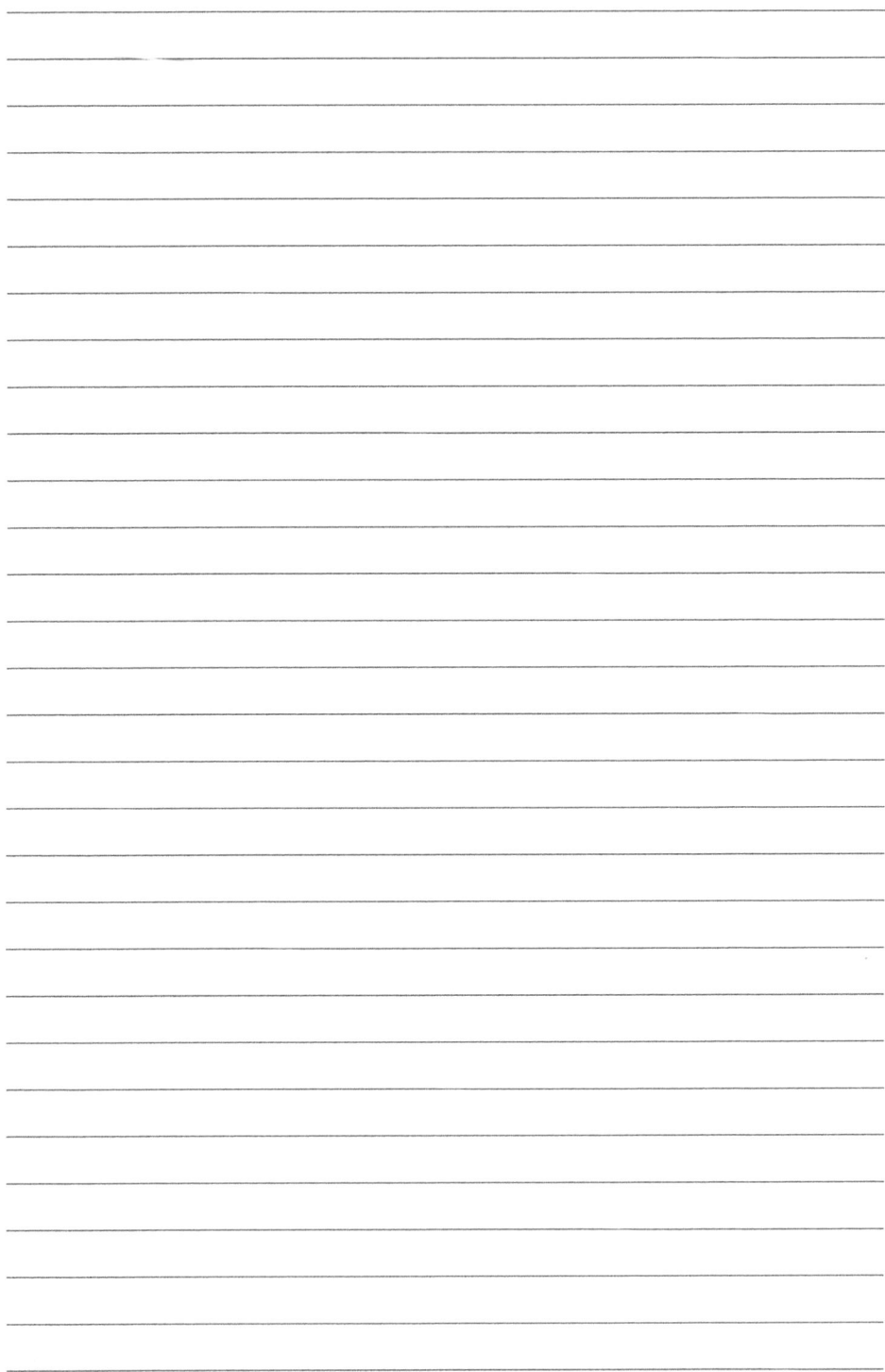

_____
_____
_____
_____
_____
_____
_____
_____
_____
_____
_____
_____
_____
_____
_____
_____
_____
_____
_____
_____
_____
_____
_____
_____
_____
_____
_____
_____
_____
_____

*"Being communicative means that you can communicate and
express your and other's ideas in a respectable way."*
— 11th Grade Student

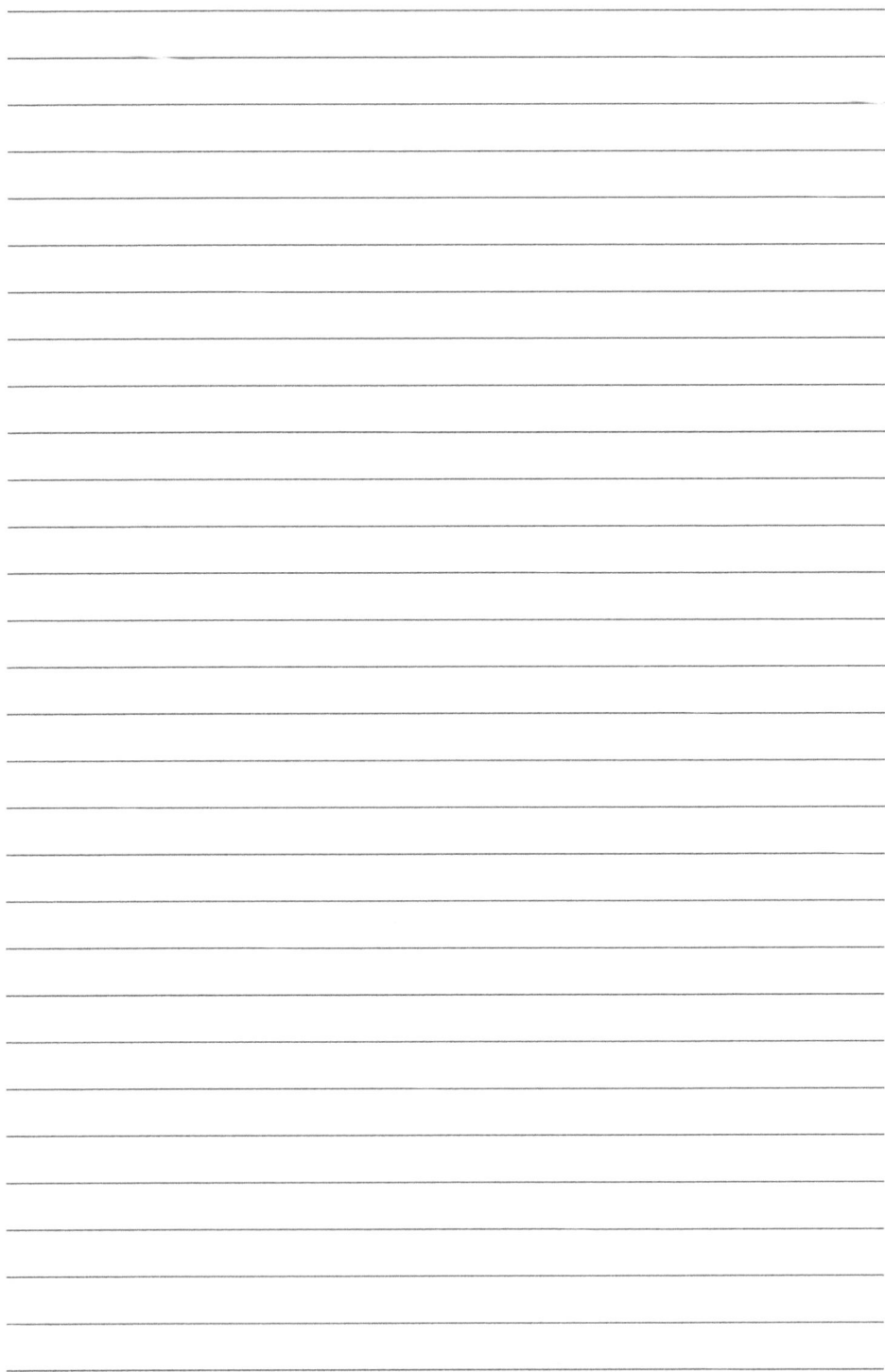

_____

_____

_____

_____

_____

_____

_____

_____

_____

_____

_____

_____

_____

_____

_____

_____

_____

_____

_____

_____

_____

_____

_____

_____

_____

_____

_____

*"[Active listeners] listen carefully to everyone's ideas
or thoughts even if you don't agree with them."*
— Fourth Grade Student

# 3

# CHANGING YOUR WORLD

Working to make a positive impact in your world

Visionary — Motivating — Encouraging — Confident

*"Whatever you do, it changes your world in a positive or negative*
*way, and it can change others' worlds too."*
— Elementary School Student

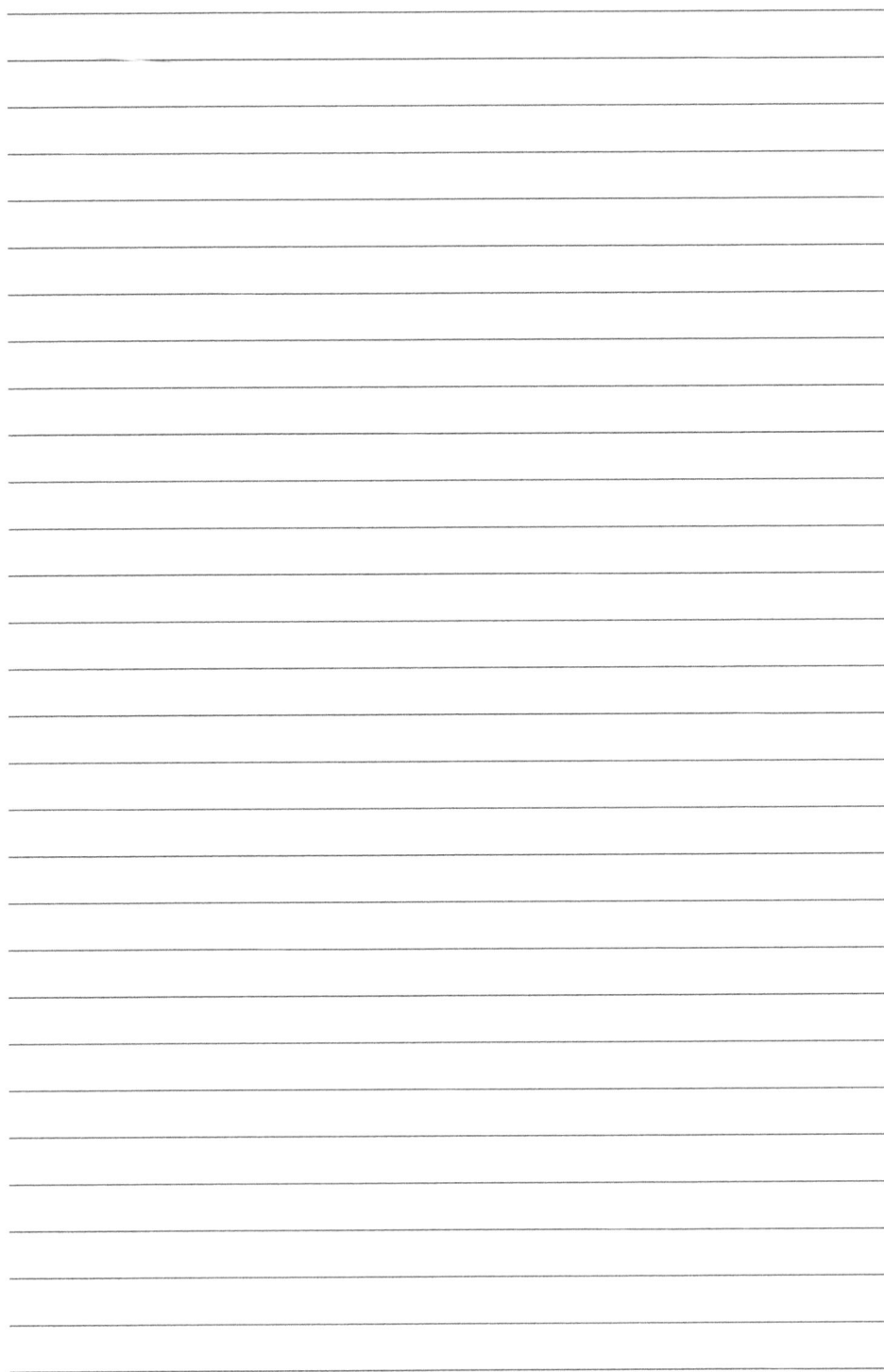

_"[Visionary means] to look ahead and think in the future. It is Martin Luther King Jr. saying 'I have a dream that all people are equal'."_

— Fourth Grade Student

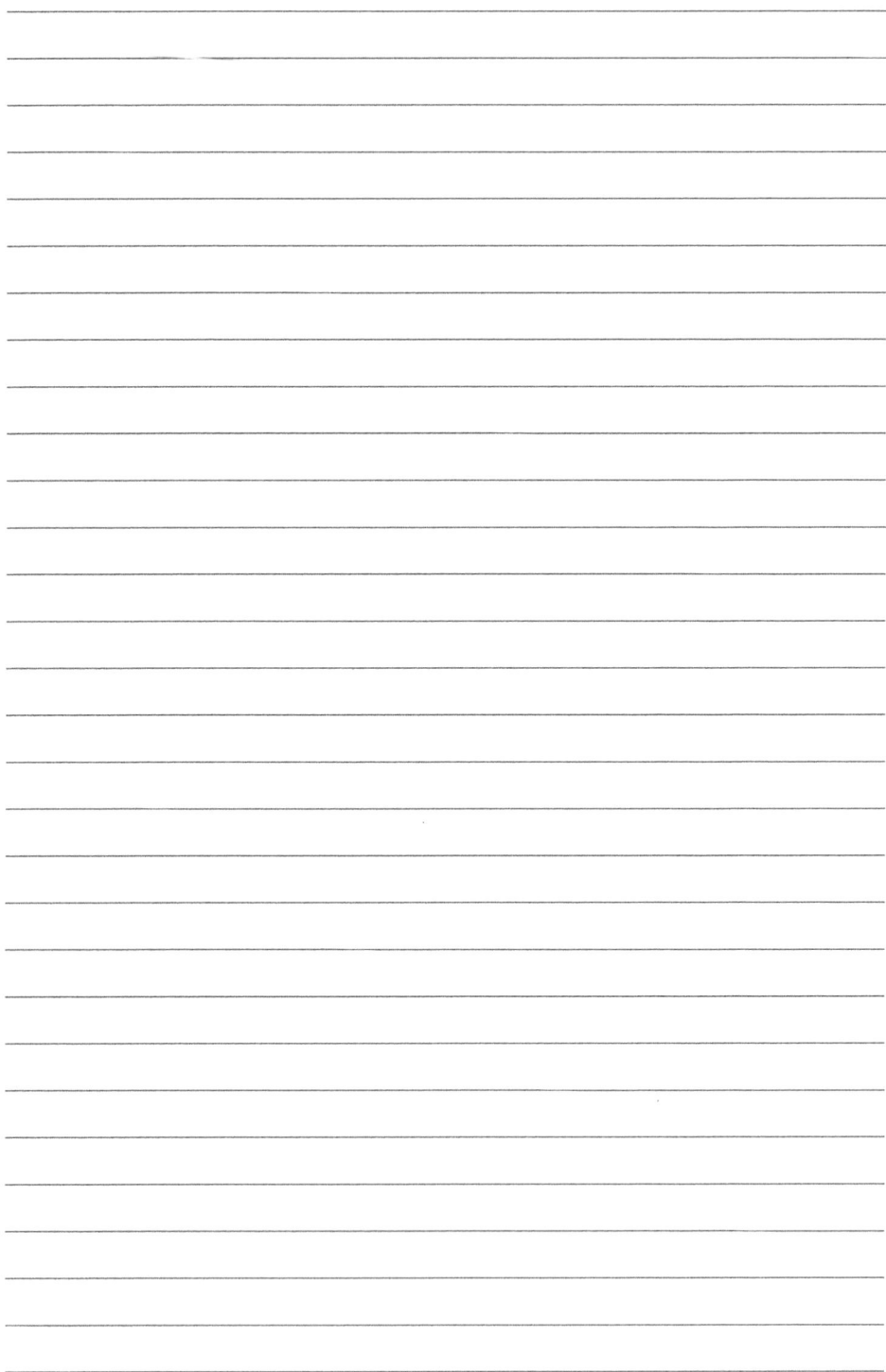

_"Visionary is applying new ideas (created by yourself or others) to make a change in the world around you. This is about learning to recognize and make use of strong imagination."_
— 11th Grade Student

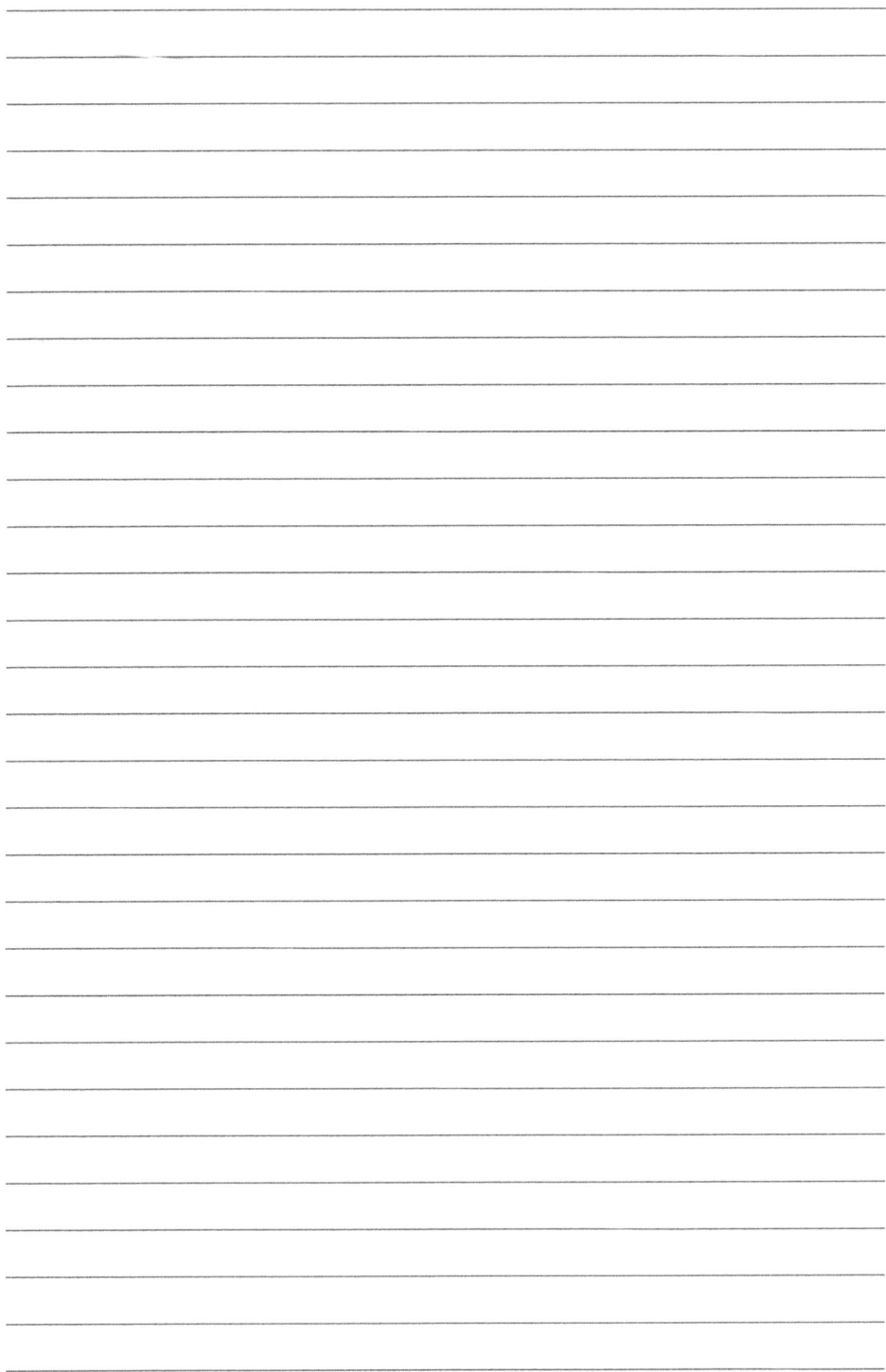

_____
_____
_____
_____
_____
_____
_____
_____
_____
_____
_____
_____
_____
_____
_____
_____
_____
_____
_____
_____
_____
_____
_____
_____
_____
_____

*"[Motivating] means knowing how to get people to work together to achieve your goal."*
— Eighth Grade Student

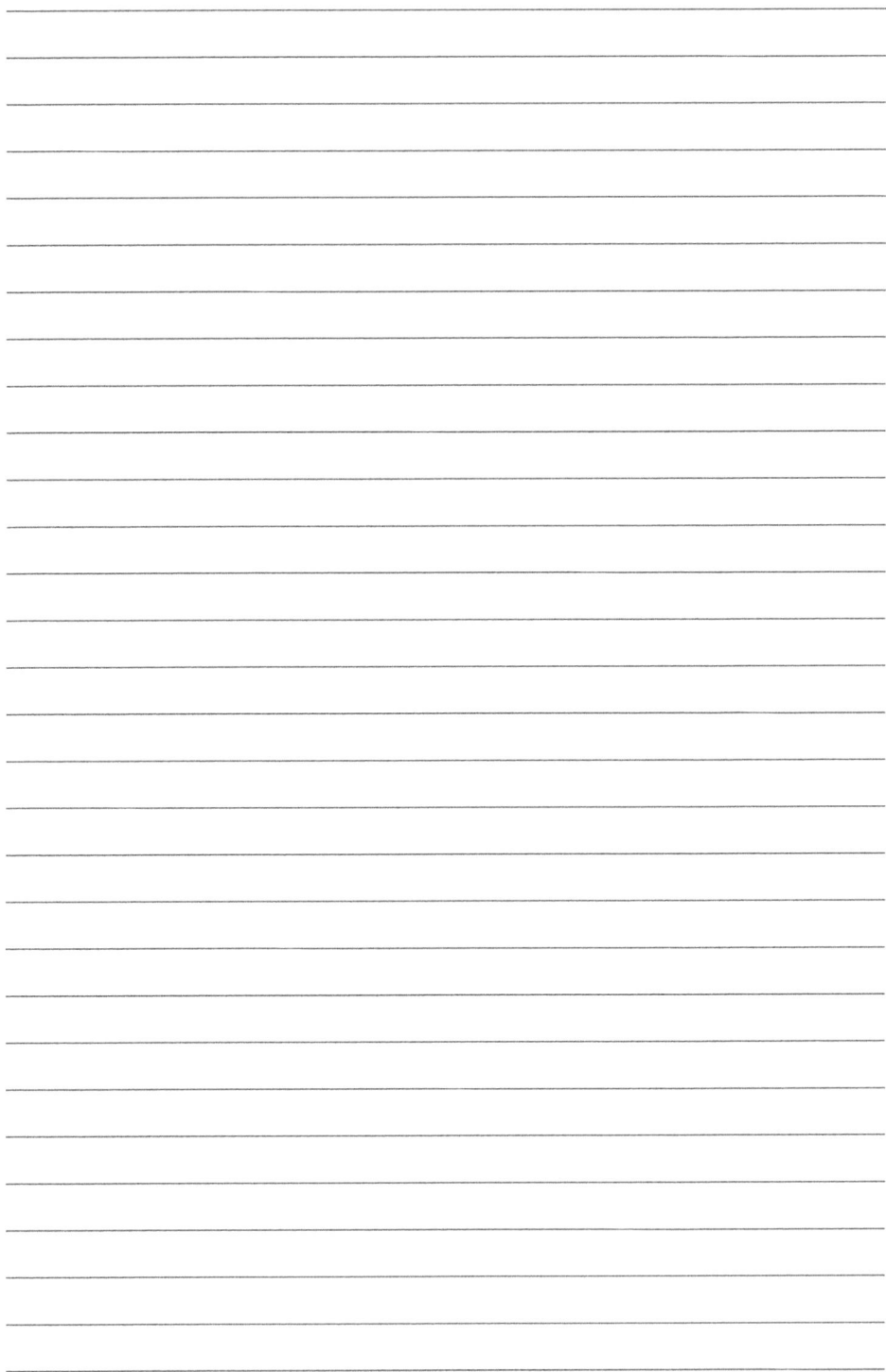

_"[Motivating] means trying to understand how others think and feel,
and even if one does not completely understand others, they listen and
communicate to reach a collaborative level."_

— 10th Grade Student

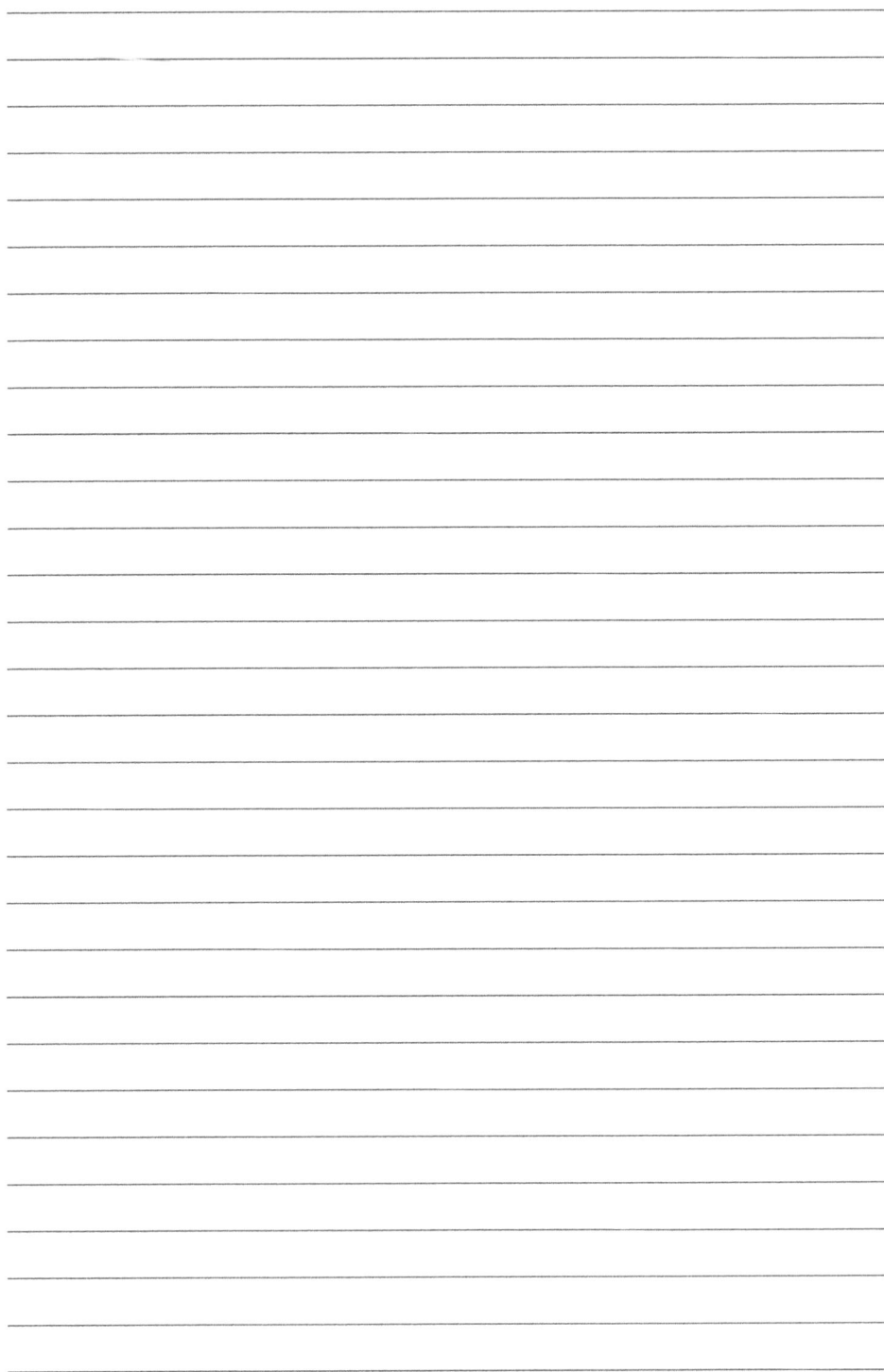

_____
_____
_____
_____
_____
_____
_____
_____
_____
_____
_____
_____
_____
_____
_____
_____
_____
_____
_____
_____
_____
_____
_____
_____
_____
_____
_____
_____
_____

*"I understand what my friends are good at and I encourage them to be leaders."*
— Fifth Grade Student

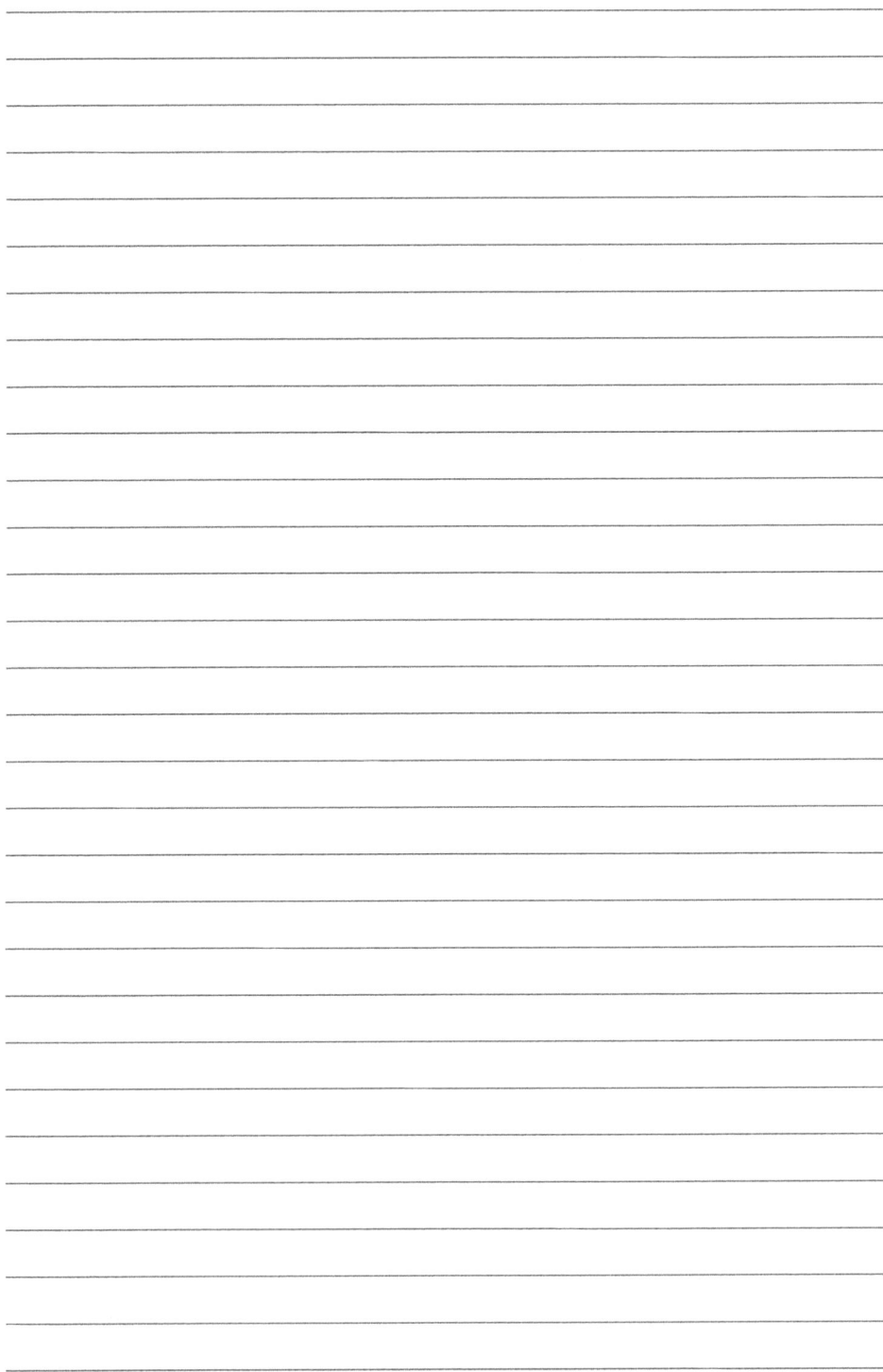

_____

_____

_____

_____

_____

_____

_____

_____

_____

_____

_____

_____

_____

_____

_____

_____

_____

_____

_____

_____

_____

_____

_____

_____

_____

*"[Encouraging] means that when you are working in a group project,
you ask people who are good at certain things (like putting together
PowerPoint presentations) to lead that part of the work."*
— 10th Grade Student

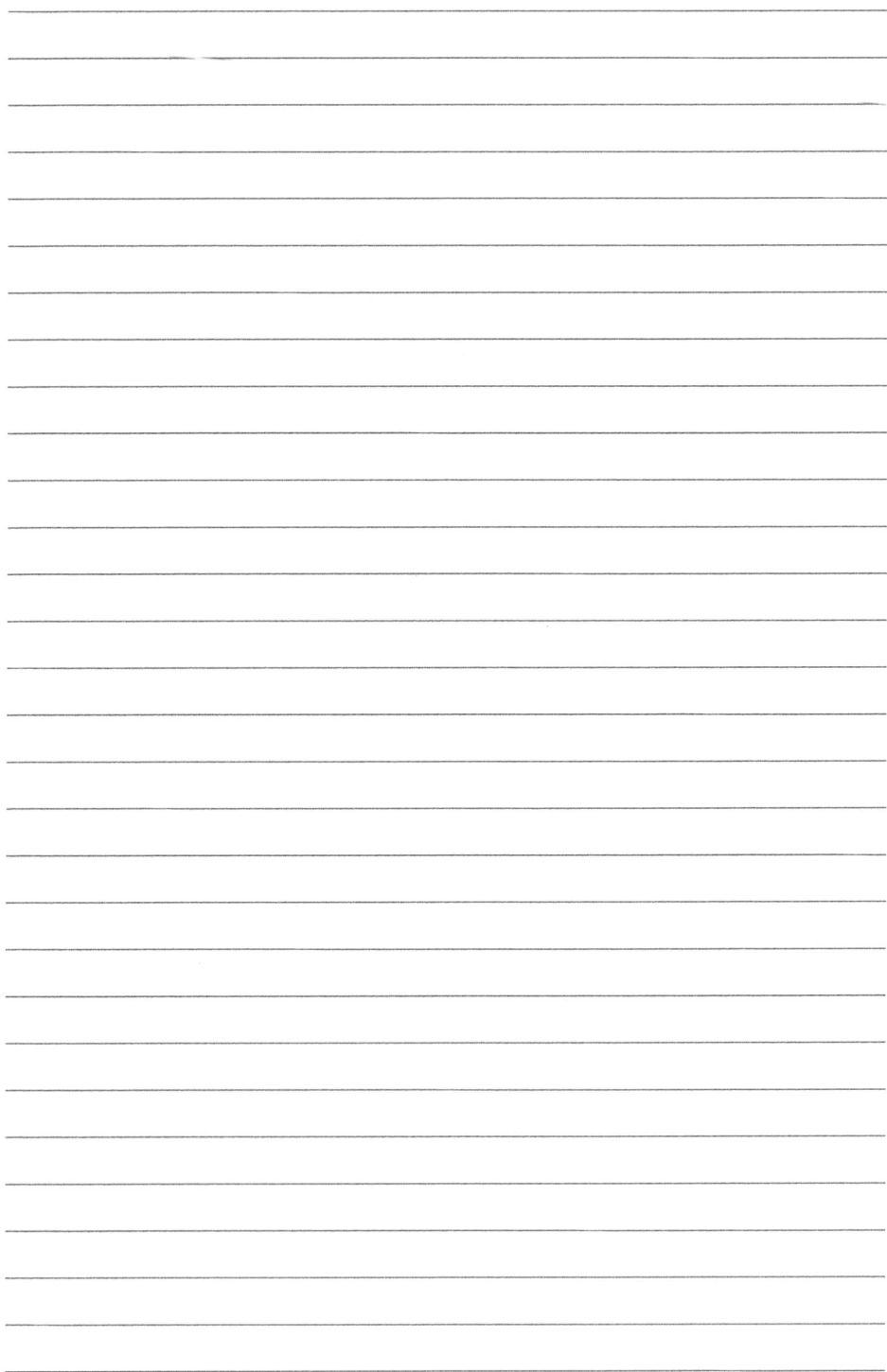

_"Being confident means being a leader without being bossy."_
— Fourth Grade Student

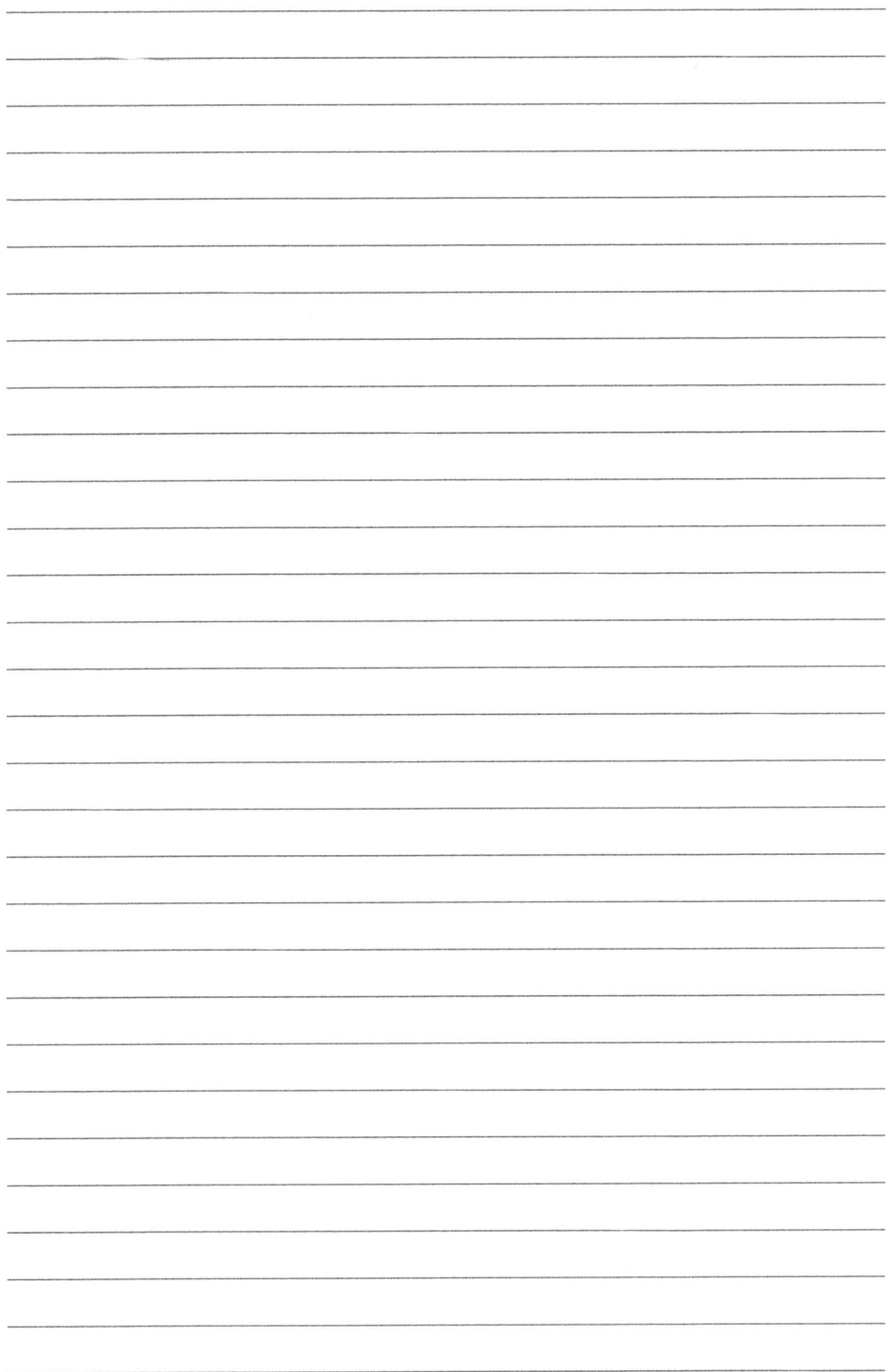

*"Being confident means believing in yourself and sharing your ideas."*
— Sixth Grade Student

www.ingramcontent.com/pod-product-compliance
Lightning Source LLC
Chambersburg PA
CBHW051125210326
41520CB00040B/7519